THE BROONS

Diary 2013

Week-to-view Diary

Vital dates for 2013

Scottish Events and Historical Dates

Scottish Words and Sayings

Broons Wisdom

Fun from the Happy Family that
makes Every Family Happy

WAVERLEY
BOOKS

Important Information

In an emergency, contact ....

....

....

Mobile.................................

Home phone..............................

Work phone.............................

Email.................................

Work email..............................

Doctor ....

Dentist................................

Polis ....

Hoose insurance no. ....

Motor insurance no. ....

Life insurance no. ....

Sweep ....

Coal man ....

Plumber................................

Boolin' Club.............................

Turn for the stairs ....

Turn at the steamie ....

Onion Johnny ....

Day for the fish van........................

Day for the rag man ....

Bin day ....

Birthdays...................................

....

....

....

....

Appointments ....

....

....

....

....

Anniversaries ....

....

....

....

....

Celebrations................................

....

....

....

....

2013

The year at a glance

JANUARY
M	T	W	T	F	S	S
	1	2	3	4	5	6
7	8	9	10	11	12	13
14	15	16	17	18	19	20
21	22	23	24	25	26	27
28	29	30	31			

FEBRUARY
M	T	W	T	F	S	S
				1	2	3
4	5	6	7	8	9	10
11	12	13	14	15	16	17
18	19	20	21	22	23	24
25	26	27	28			

MARCH
M	T	W	T	F	S	S
				1	2	3
4	5	6	7	8	9	10
11	12	13	14	15	16	17
18	19	20	21	22	23	24
25	26	27	28	29	30	31

APRIL
M	T	W	T	F	S	S
1	2	3	4	5	6	7
8	9	10	11	12	13	14
15	16	17	18	19	20	21
22	23	24	25	26	27	28
29	30					

MAY
M	T	W	T	F	S	S
		1	2	3	4	5
6	7	8	9	10	11	12
13	14	15	16	17	18	19
20	21	22	23	24	25	26
27	28	29	30	31		

JUNE
M	T	W	T	F	S	S
					1	2
3	4	5	6	7	8	9
10	11	12	13	14	15	16
17	18	19	20	21	22	23
24	25	26	27	28	29	30

JULY
M	T	W	T	F	S	S
1	2	3	4	5	6	7
8	9	10	11	12	13	14
15	16	17	18	19	20	21
22	23	24	25	26	27	28
29	30	31				

AUGUST
M	T	W	T	F	S	S
			1	2	3	4
5	6	7	8	9	10	11
12	13	14	15	16	17	18
19	20	21	22	23	24	25
26	27	28	29	30	31	

SEPTEMBER
M	T	W	T	F	S	S
30						1
2	3	4	5	6	7	8
9	10	11	12	13	14	15
16	17	18	19	20	21	22
23	24	25	26	27	28	29

OCTOBER
M	T	W	T	F	S	S
	1	2	3	4	5	6
7	8	9	10	11	12	13
14	15	16	17	18	19	20
21	22	23	24	25	26	27
28	29	30	31			

NOVEMBER
M	T	W	T	F	S	S
				1	2	3
4	5	6	7	8	9	10
11	12	13	14	15	16	17
18	19	20	21	22	23	24
25	26	27	28	29	30	

DECEMBER
M	T	W	T	F	S	S
30	31					1
2	3	4	5	6	7	8
9	10	11	12	13	14	15
16	17	18	19	20	21	22
23	24	25	26	27	28	29

OOR FREENDS The Broons

 Paw Broon has worn the same suit since 1936. He drinks his tea out of the saucer. Has rarely been seen to do the housework unless forced (or if Maw punishes him for misbehaving). An affectionate and well-meaning father and husband, but he's not the brightest. He and his faither can get into worse trouble than the bairns.

 Maw Broon is rarely seen without her pinny on, unless she is going out (to the pictures with her lassies or to the Women's Guild), when she wears a coat and sometimes a hat. A culinary queen when it comes to clootie dumpling, mince and tatties and Black Bun. Has worn her hair in a bun since 1936. Her brusque exterior belies a love for jujube sweeties and a soppy film. A long-suffering and loving (if sometimes a bit nippy) manager of the family.

 Unusually tall and skinny for a Scotsman, Hen Broon has been the subject of much graffiti in his time. Usually wears a striped suit and a bowler hat unless he's having his tea. Joined the army during World War II. Has had varied success with the ladies, who often have to stand on the close stairs to be able to reach him to give him a wee kiss. He has a bottomless stomach for one so lanky.

 Joe Broon is shorter and stockier than Hen. He and his brother are good pals and they love the outdoors and their holidays at the But an' Ben. They like a guid party and Joe can contribute to this by playing the bagpipes and the accordion. Like Hen, he served his country during the war. Despite Hen and Joe always being on the look out for a click, they rarely try to be fashionable. They were once seen in duffle coats.

 Maggie Broon is the stylish, glamorous one. Never seen without her lipstick, even at the tattie howkin'. Since 1936, she and her sister Daph have always tried to keep up with the current fashions and hairstyles. She and Daph get on very well. There were never such devoted sisters ... unless in competition for an eligible bachelor. In 1977 she was engaged to Dave McKay. Whatever happened to him? None of the other Broons offspring have come as close to marriage.

Though plump and less glamorous than her sister Maggie, Daphne Broon does her best to get dolled up and has had her share of lumbers (none of them oil paintings though). Her diets receive no support from the family, and she's the butt of many a joke. When a letter or package arrives addressed to "Miss Broon", confusion reigns (though you can bet it's probably for the Bairn). Unlike the other Broons, Maggie and Daph have had varied hairstyles over the years. You can often tell what decade it is from Daphne's hairdo.

Horace Broon is quite cheerful for someone who is constantly tormented by his younger brothers and has been in short trousers for over 70 years. He is the brains of the family. Before the Internet was invented, if the Broons needed information they just asked Horace. His varied attempts to bring some culture to Glebe Street invariably end in frustration.

The youngest Broon, The Bairn, often manages to appear to be the most mature member of the family. Like a mini version of Maw, she likes to tell-off her siblings, and sometimes her parents, for bad behaviour. She loves her dollies and her pram. She and Granpaw are best pals and she prefers to spend time with him than bairns her own age. Her misinterpretation of what she overhears from the adults is often the cause of the family's trademark mix-ups.

Perhaps we can put the sometimes unruly behaviour of the Broons Twins down to them being deficient of first names - they are only ever called The Twins, or sometimes Ae Twin and the Ither Twin. Fond of fighting, catties, bogies, fitba in the street, sliding and scrumping aipples. They don't like lassies, bath night, housework, school or sharing.

Granpaw Broon can be more trouble than all the children put together. Always on the look out for a free feed or getting his washing done, he may not live at Glebe Street but he might as well. Look out for his portrait on the wall in many of the strips reacting to the antics of the family. He likes his pipe, clootie dumplin', a dram, granny sookers, the boolin', his shed, and gossiping with his cronies.

Read The Broons every week in
The Sunday Post

Events Across Scotland

ROYAL HIGHLAND SHOW, INGLISTON – JUNE

T IN THE PARK, BALADO AIRFIELD – JULY

CEÒL CHOLASA, COLONSAY – SEPTEMBER

UP-HELLY-AA, LERWICK SHETLAND – JANUARY

BURNING OF THE CLAVIE, BURGHEAD – JANUARY

HEBRIDEAN CELTIC FESTIVAL STORNOWAY – JULY

BARRA FEST BARRA – JULY

TIREE WAVE CLASSIC – OCTOBER

EDINBURGH FESTIVAL – AUGUST

EDINBURGH MILITARY TATTOO – AUGUST

EDINBURGH MOONWALK – JUNE

BELTANE FESTIVAL, EDINBURGH – APRIL 30

WICKERMAN FESTIVAL, KIRCUDBRIGHT – JULY

WIGTOWN BOOK FESTIVAL – MAY

LANARK LANIMERS DAY – JUNE

SEE NEXT PAGE FOR THE MANY GALA DAYS AND COMMON RIDINGS TO BE FOUND IN SCOTLAND

WORLD STONE SKIMMING CHAMPIONSHIPS EASDALE ISLAND – SEPTEMBER

AYE WRITE FESTIVAL, GLASGOW – MARCH

BBC GOOD FOOD SHOW, GLASGOW – OCTOBER

NOTABLE DATES AND MOVABLE FEASTS 2013 ᴅᴀᴇ ʏᴇ ᴍᴇᴀɴ pichics?

January 1	Ne'erday, holiday
January 2	Holiday (Scot, NZ)
January 14	Makar Sankranti (Hindu Festival)
January 25	Burns Night
February 12	Shrove Tuesday
February 13	Ash Wednesday, Lent begins
February 14	St Valentine's Day
March 1	St David's Day (Wales)
March 10	Mothering Sunday (UK and R of I)
March 18	St Patrick's Day holiday (R of I, NI)
March 24	Palm Sunday
March 26	Passover begins (from sunset of 25)
March 27	Holi (Hindu festival)
March 28	Maundy Thursday
March 29	Good Friday, holiday (except R of I)
March 30	Easter Saturday, Lent ends
March 31	Easter Sunday.
	British Summer Time (BST) begins.
	Irish Standard Time (IST) begins
April 1	Easter Monday, holiday (except parts of Scot).
	April Fools' Day, Huntigowk
April 2	Passover ends
April 23	St George's Day (England)
May 1	Beltane
May 6	Bank Holiday (UK, R of I)
May 12	Mother's Day (Aus, Can, NZ, US)
May 15	Shavuot (Jewish holiday, from sunset of 14)
May 19	Pentecost
May 26	Trinity Sunday
May 27	Spring Bank Holiday (UK)
June 3	June Bank Holiday (R of I)
June 16	Father's Day (Can, R of I, UK, US)
June 21	Summer Solstice
June 23	Midsummer E'en (St John's Eve)
June 24	Midsummer Day, St John the Baptist Day
June 29	Edinburgh Trades Holiday begins (till 14)
July 9	Ramadan begins (from sunset of 8)
July 13	Glasgow Fair begins (till 27)
July 15	St Swithun's Day
July 16	Tisha B'Av, Jewish holiday (from sunset of 15)
August 3	Laylat al-Qadr, Muslim Night of Power
August 5	Summer Bank Holiday (Scot, R of I)
August 8	Eid ul-Fitr (Ramadan ends)
August 26	Summer Bank Holiday (UK except Scot)
September 1	Father's Day (Aus, NZ)
September 5	Rosh Hashanah (Jewish New Year (from sunset of 4)
September 9	Ganesh Chaturthi (Hindu festival)
September 14	Yom Kippur (Jewish Day of Atonement, from sunset of 13)
September 16	Edinburgh Autumn Holiday
September 27	Glasgow September Weekend begins (till 30)
September 29	Michaelmas Day
October 5	Navratri (Hindu festival)
October 13	Navratri ends

October 14	Thanksgiving (Can)
October 15	Eid al-Adha (Muslim Festival of Sacrifice)
October 27	British Summer Time (BST) ends.
	Irish Standard Time (IST) ends
October 28	October Bank Holiday (R of I)
October 31	Halloween, Samhain, Celtic New Year
November 1	All Saints' Day
November 2	All Souls' Day
November 3	Diwali (Hindu Festival of Lights)
November 5	Muharram begins, first month of Islamic calendar (from sunset of 4).
	Guy Fawkes Night (UK)
November 7	Diwali ends
November 10	Remembrance Sunday
November 11	Remembrance Day
November 28	Hanukkah begins (from sunset of 27).
	Thanksgiving (US)
November 30	St Andrew's Day
December 1	Advent Sunday
December 2	St Andrew's Day, holiday (Scot)
December 3	Muharram ends
December 5	Hanukkah ends
December 21	Winter Solstice
December 24	Christmas Eve
December 25	Christmas Day, holiday
December 26	Boxing Day, holiday
December 31	New Year's Eve.
	Hogmanay (Scot)

SCOTTISH GALA DAYS, GAMES AND FESTIVALS 2013

January 1	Kirkwall New Year Ba' Game, Orkney.	July 27	Callander, Dufftown, Halkirk, Lochaber,
	The Loony Dook, South Queensferry		Strathconon Highland Games.
January 11	Burning of the Clavie, Burghead, Moray		Countryside Festival, Glamis Castle (till 28)
January 29	Up-Helly-Aa, Lerwick, Shetland	July 28	St Andrews Highland Games
February 12	Fastern's E'en Ba', Duns		Lauder Common Riding (till Aug 3)
February 14	Callant's Ba', Jedburgh	July 31	Arisaig Highland Games
March	Aye Write! Festival, Glasgow	August	Edinburgh International Festival and Fringe
March 1	Whuppity Scoorie, Lanark	August 2	Dornoch Highland Games.
April 30	Beltane Fires on Calton Hill in Edinburgh	August 3	Aberlour & Strathspey, Brodick, Inverkeithing,
May 12	Gourock Highland Games		Mey, Newtonmore Highland Games.
May 25	Blackford, West Lothian Highland Games		Lauder Common Riding Day
May 25-26	Atholl Gathering and Highland Games	August 4	Bridge Of Allan, Montrose Highland Games
June 1	Cornhill, Shotts Highland Games.		Coldstream Civic Week begins (till 10)
June 2	Carrick Lowland Games (Girvan).	August 7	Isle Of Skye, Killin Highland Games
	Markinch Highland Games	August 8	Ballater Highland Games.
June 6	Lanimer Day, Lanark		Tain Highland Gathering.
June 7	Hawick Common Riding (till June 8)		Coldstream Flodden Cavalcade
	West Linton Whipman (till June 8)	August 9	Assynt, Atholl & Breadalbane Highland Games.
June 8	Bearsden & Milngavie Highland Games		The Burryman, South Queensferry
June 9	Ardrossan, Forfar Highland Games.	August 10	Ferry Fair Festival, South Queensferry,
	Guid Nychburris Festival, Dumfries (till 15)		Abernethy, Dundonald, North Berwick,
June 14	Selkirk Common Riding Day		Strathpeffer Highland Games.
June 15	Lesmahagow, Newburgh, Oldmeldrum Games		The Borders Gathering begins (till 11)
June 16	City of Aberdeen Highland Games.	August 11	Cortachy, Perth Highland Games
	Peebles Beltane Week begins (till 22).	August 17	Bute, Helmsdale & District, Rannoch, Nairn
	Melrose Festival begins (till 23)		Highland Games.
June 18	Riding of Linlithgow Marches		Sanquhar Riding of the Marches
June 20	Royal Highland Show begins (till 23)	August 18	Caithness, Crieff, Glenfinnan Highland Games
June 22	Linlithgow Gala Day.	August 22	Argyllshire Gathering (Includes Oban Games)
	Peebles Beltane Festival.	August 24	Lonach Highland Gathering and Games
June 23	Braw Lads Gathering, Galashiels (till 30)	August 25	Grantown-On-Spey Highland Games
June 29	Braw Lads Day, Galashiels.	August 29	Cowal Highland Gathering begins (till 31)
	Ceres, Drumtochty Highland Games	August 31	Birnam, Glenurquhart, Invergordon, Strathardle
June 30	Duns Summer Festival begins (till July 6)		Highland Games
July 3	Kenmore Highland Games	August 31	Largs Viking Festival begins (till Sep 8)
July 4	Thornton Highland Games	September 1	Blairgowrie & Rattray Highland Games
July 6	Annan Riding of the Marches.	September 7	Braemar Gathering
	Forres, Glengarry, Gairloch, Luss Highland Games.	September 8	Peebles Highland Games
July 7	Cupar Highland Games	September 14	Pitlochry Highland Games
July 12	Jethart (Jedburgh) Callant's Festival Day.	September 21	Invercharron Traditional Highland Games
July 13	Alva, Morvern Highland Games	December 25	Kirkwall Christmas Ba' Game, Orkney
July	T in the Park (usu. second week of July)	December 31	Biggar's Bonfire.
July 14	Stirling Highland Games		Comrie Flambeaux Procession.
July 15	Burntisland Highland Games		The Stonehaven Fireball Ceremony
July 16	Inveraray Traditional Highland Games		
July 18	Mull Highland Games		
July 19	St Ronan's Border Games (till 20)		
July 20	City of Inverness, Lochcarron, Lochearnhead,		
	Taynuilt, Tomintoul Highland Games.		
	Comrie Fortnight begins (till Aug 3).		
	Kelso Civic Week begins (till 27).		
July 21	Stonehaven Highland Games.		
	Castle Douglas Civic Week begins (till 27).		
July 26	Durness Highland Gathering.		
	Langholm Common Riding		

Event dates above and marked thus † in the diary were still to be confirmed at time of press and may be subject to change. Contact organisers or see individual event websites for details.

A FAMILY TREE OF THE SCOTTISH MONARCHY

Wi comments by the Twins and Horace

Alpin

did King Alpin invent muesli?

these are kings of the Picts

KENNETH I
843–858

DONALD I
858–862

CONSTANTINE I
862–877

AODH
877–878

daughter
m. Run, king of the Britons

DONALD II *'the madman!'*
889–900

CONSTANTINE II *abdicated to become a monk*
900–943

EOCHAID (?)
878–889

GIRIC (?)
878–889

these are kings of Alba

MALCOLM I
943–954

INDULF
954–962

DUBH
962–967

KENNETH II
971–995

CULEN
967–971

Dubh was killed by Culen who took over as king — that's no' fair!

killed by Malcolm II

KENNETH III
?997–1005

MALCOLM II
1005–1034

CONSTANTINE III
995–997

GIRIC (?)
?–1005

Boete

We thocht he wis made up

Findlaec m. Donada ?
d. 1020

Bethoc
m. Crinan, Abbot of Dunkeld

daughter
m. Sigurd

Rained 29 years

Gillacomgan m. Gruoch m. **MACBETH**
d. 1032   1040–1057

DUNCAN I
1034–1040

Thorfinn

LULACH
1057–1058

Canmore means big heid

(1) Ingibiorg m. **MALCOLM III** m.
Widow of   (Canmore)
Thorfinn   1058–1093

(2) Margaret
Sister of Edgar
Atheling

DONALD III
Donald Bane, 'The Fair'
1093–1094
1094–1097

jings, Lulach wisna aroond for long

DUNCAN II
1094

EDGAR
'The Valiant'
1097–1107

ALEXANDER I
'The Fierce'
1107–1124

DAVID I
'The Saint'
1124–1153

known as Saint Margaret

Henry, Prince of Scotland d. 1152

MALCOLM IV
'The Maiden'
1153–1165

WILLIAM
'The Lion'
1165–1214

David,
Earl of
Huntingdon

fell aff a cliff on the way to see his wummin

ALEXANDER II
1214–1249

ALEXANDER III
1249–1286

Margaret m.
Alan of
Galloway

Isabella
m. Robert de
Brus

Ada
m. Henry de
Hastynges

Margaret m.
Eric II of
Norway
d. 1283

Alexander,
Prince of
Scotland
d. 1284

Devorgilla m.
John de
Balliol

Robert de Brus
'the Competitor'

MARGARET
'The Maid of
Norway'
1286–1290

there's no too many lassies in this tree

**JOHN
BALLIOL**
1292–1296

Edward Balliol

Robert de Brus
m. Countess of Carrick

ROBERT I
'The Bruce'
1306–1329

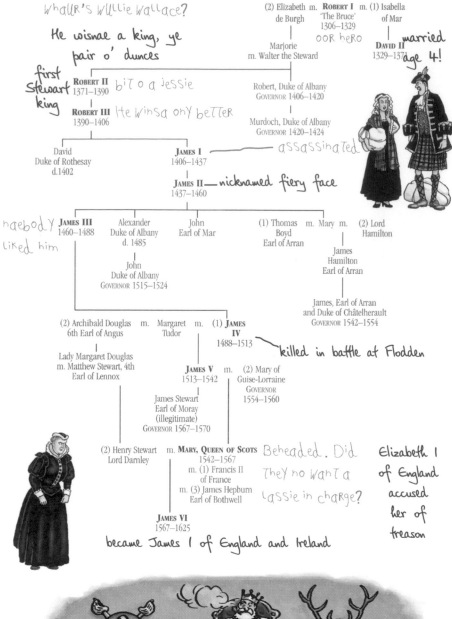

whaUR's wUllie wallace?

He wisnae a king, ye pair o' dunces

(2) Elizabeth m. **ROBERT I** m. (1) Isabella
de Burgh 'The Bruce' of Mar
1306–1329
OOR heRO

Marjorie
m. Walter the Steward

DAVID II *married*
1329–137*age 4!*

first Stewart king

ROBERT II *biT o a jessie*
1371–1390

Robert, Duke of Albany
GOVERNOR 1406–1420

ROBERT III *He winsa ony beTTer*
1390–1406

Murdoch, Duke of Albany
GOVERNOR 1420–1424

David
Duke of Rothesay
d.1402

JAMES I —————— *assassinaTed*
1406–1437

JAMES II — *nicknamed fiery face*
1437–1460

naebody liked him

JAMES III
1460–1488

Alexander
Duke of Albany
d. 1485

John
Earl of Mar

(1) Thomas m. Mary m. (2) Lord
Boyd Hamilton
Earl of Arran

James
Hamilton
Earl of Arran

John
Duke of Albany
GOVERNOR 1515–1524

James, Earl of Arran
and Duke of Châtelherault
GOVERNOR 1542–1554

(2) Archibald Douglas m. Margaret m. (1) **JAMES**
6th Earl of Angus Tudor **IV**
1488–1513

killed in battle at Flodden

Lady Margaret Douglas
m. Matthew Stewart, 4th
Earl of Lennox

JAMES V m. (2) Mary of
1513–1542 Guise-Lorraine
GOVERNOR
1554–1560

James Stewart
Earl of Moray
(illegitimate)
GOVERNOR 1567–1570

(2) Henry Stewart m. **MARY, QUEEN OF SCOTS**
Lord Darnley 1542–1567
m. (1) Francis II
of France
m. (3) James Hepburn
Earl of Bothwell

Beheaded. Did they no wanT a lassie in chaRge?

Elizabeth I of England accused her of treason

JAMES VI
1567–1625

became James I of England and Ireland

CLOTHING SIZES AND CONVERSIONS

Women's clothing sizes

UK	4	6	8	10	12	14	16	18	20	22	24
US	0	2	4	6	8	10	12	14	16	18	20
EU	34	36	38	40	42	44	46	48	50	52	54

Girls' dresses and coats

UK	3	5	7	9	11	13	15	17
US	1	3	5	7	9	11	13	15
EU	28	30	32	34	36	38	40	42

Men's suits, jumpers and coats

UK / US	38	40	42	44	46	48	50	52	54
EU	48	50	52	54	56	58	60	62	64

Men's shirts

	S	M	L	XL	XXL	3XL	4XL
UK / US	14-14½	15-15½	16-16½	17-17½	18-18½	19-19½	20-20½
EU	36	38-40	42-44	46-48	50-52	54-56	58-60

Shoes

Ladies

UK	2	2.5	3	3.5	4	4.5	5	5.5	6	6.5	7	7.5	8
US	4.5	5	5.5	6	6.5	7	7.5	8	8.5	9	9.5	10	10.5
EU	34	35	35.5	36	37	37.5	38	38.5	39	39.5	40	41	42

The Family's Clothes Sizes

Paw
bonnet: 7 3/8
collar: 16"

Me
dress: never
you mind
hat: 8

Joe
hat: 7 3/8
collar: 18

Maggie
hat: 7
dress: 12

Bairn
bonnet: 50cm,
or age 3
dress: age 3
shoes: 1

boots: 7   shoes: 8   shoes: 10   shoes: 4

CLOTHING SIZES AND CONVERSIONS

Shoes

Men

UK	5	5.5	6	6.5	7	7.5	8	8.5	9	9.5	10	10.5	11	11.5	12	
US	5.5	6	6.5	7	7.5	8	8.5	9	9.5	10	10.5	11	11.5	12	12.5	
EU	38	38.7	39.3	40	40.5	41	42	42.5	43	44	44.5	45	46	46.5	47	

Girls

UK	8	8.5	9	9.5	10	10.5	11	11.5	12	12.5	13	13.5	1	1.5	2	2.5
US	8.5	9	9.5	10	10.5	11	11.5	12	13.5	13	13.5	1	1.5	2	2.5	3
EU	26	26.5	27	27.5	28	28.5	29	30	30.5	31	31.5	32.2	33	33.5	34	35

Boys

UK	11	11.5	12	12.5	13	13.5	1	1.5	2	2.5	3	3.5	4	4.5
US	11.5	12	12.5	13	13.5	1	1.5	2	2.5	3	3.5	4	4.5	5
EU	29	29.7	30.5	31	31.5	33	33.5	34	34.7	35	35.5	36	37	37.5

Hat sizes

UK	$6^3/_8$	$6\frac{1}{2}$	$6^5/_8$	$6\frac{3}{4}$	$6^7/_8$	7	$7^1/_8$	$7\frac{1}{4}$	$7^3/_8$	$7\frac{1}{2}$	$7^5/_8$
USA	$6\frac{1}{2}$	$6^5/_8$	$6\frac{3}{4}$	$6^7/_8$	7	$7^1/_8$	$7\frac{1}{4}$	$7^3/_8$	$7\frac{1}{2}$	$7^5/_8$	$7\frac{3}{4}$
Inches	$20\frac{1}{2}$	$20^7/_8$	$21\frac{1}{4}$	$21^5/_8$	22	$22\frac{1}{2}$	$22^7/_8$	$23\frac{1}{4}$	$23^5/_8$	24	$24\frac{1}{2}$
Centimetres	52	53	54	55	56	57	58	59	60	61	62

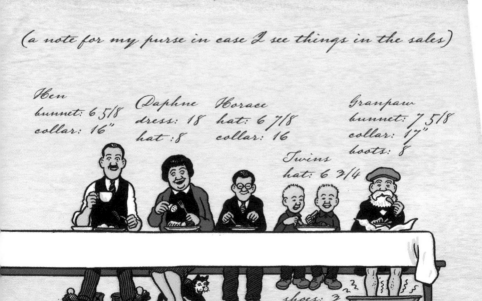

(a note for my purse in case I see things in the sales)

Hen
bunnet: 6 5/8
collar: 16"

Daphne
dress: 18
hat: 8

Horace
hat: 6 7/8
collar: 16

Granpaw
bunnet: 7 5/8
collar: 17"
boots: 8

Twins
hat: 6 3/4
shoes: 3

boots: 12   shoes: 8   boots: 5   basin: 18"

January

The Twins new Year
Resolooshuns

1 | dinna get caught

2 | spend less on sweeties
(steal Horace's)

3 | keep fit (so Paw cannae
catch us, see Resolooshun 7)

4 | do weekend home work on a
friday (gives plenty of time
to lose it)

5 | eat more greens (starting
wi Granpaw's secret stash
o soor plooms)

№ 9 MACDUFF'S
SCOTTISH FOODS OF QUALITY

400 g / 14 oz tin condensed milk 1 kg / 2 ¼ lb sugar
125 g / 4 oz salted butter 1 cup full-cream milk

Melt butter over a low heat. Add milk and sugar and stir
until sugar has mostly dissolved. Add condensed milk and
turn up heat to reach a slow boil. Simmer for 20 mins,
stirring continuously. Let mixture reach 118°C. If you
don't have a thermometer look out for a change in colour
– mixture should turn darker (take care not to burn).
Test mixture for hardness after about 18 mins by drop-
ping it from a spoon into cold water and see if you can
pick it up and roll into a ball. Remove from heat and beat
mixture till it starts to harden but is still pourable. Pour
into a baking tray lined with baking paper. Score into fingers while it's still warm. Leave to cool.

The "Brownlee" Tablet

The Twins Burns night tips
Burns night tips can be made by
helping clear up the dinner dishes
while the older folk enjoy a
'Refreshmint'. The more 'Refreshmint'
enjoyed, the more jenerus they become

DECEMBER 2012/JANUARY 2013

MONDAY

31 Hogmanay

Happy new Year
A bottle of ginger beer
And a skelp roond The ear

TUESDAY

1
Ne'erday, holiday.
Kirkwall New Year Ba' Game, Orkney.
The Loony Dook, South Queensferry.
Boys' Walk, Dufftown

First Footing tae
be done!

WEDNESDAY

2 Holiday (Scot; NZ)

THURSDAY

3

FRIDAY

4

SATURDAY

5 Twelfth Night

SUNDAY

Mind an' tak' the tree doon

6
Epiphany or Three Kings Day.
Birth of David Dale, founder of New Lanark, businessman and philanthropist, 1739

bairn, bairnie: child.

JANUARY 2013

MONDAY	
7	Handsel Monday, the first Monday of the year; tips or gifts were given. Founding of University of Glasgow, 1451. Death of Allan Ramsay, poet, 1758
TUESDAY	
8	Death of Edgar, King of Scots, 1107
WEDNESDAY	
9	
THURSDAY	
10	Death of Margaret MacDonald Mackintosh, artist, 1933
FRIDAY	
11	Burning of the Clavie, Burghead, Moray
SATURDAY	
12	Old Gaelic New Year's Day
SUNDAY	
13	Death of Mary Slessor, missionary, 1915

chitterin': shivering.

JANUARY 2013

MONDAY

14 Holiday (NZ: Southland).
Makar Sankranti, Hindu festival

TUESDAY

15

WEDNESDAY

16 Acts of Union passed, 1707

THURSDAY

17 Battle of Falkirk Muir, 1746

FRIDAY

18

SATURDAY

19 Birth of James Watt, engineer, 1736

SUNDAY

20

fitba: football.

MONDAY

21

Birthday of Martin Luther King, Jr., holiday (US).
Holiday (NZ: Wellington)

TUESDAY

22

WEDNESDAY

23

THURSDAY

24

FRIDAY

25

Burns Night.
Birth of Robert Burns, poet, 1759

SATURDAY

26

SUNDAY

27

Holocaust Memorial Day

faimily: family.

MONDAY

28
Australia Day, holiday (Aus).
Holiday (NZ: Auckland)

TUESDAY

29
Up-Helly-Aa, fire festival, Lerwick, Shetland

WEDNESDAY

30

THURSDAY

31
Death of Prince Charles Edward Stuart, 1788

FRIDAY

1
Imbolc or St Brigid's Day, Celtic festival marking the beginning of Spring.
Birth of Muriel Spark, writer, 1918

SATURDAY

2
Candlemas, old quarter day (now 28th).
Groundhog Day (Can, US)

SUNDAY

3

"Reckless youth makes youthful age."

February

Roses aRe Red
VioleTs aRe blUe

SUgaR is SweeT
WhaT happened To YoU?

Roses aRe Red
VioleTs aRe blUe
A face Like YoURS
belongs
in a Zoo

PosTie PosTie
Hen's so Thin
YoU michT be
mistaKen and
Think he's noT in.

Crêpe-Style Pancakes

Highland Pantry
73
RECIPE CARDS

100 g plain flour
250 ml milk
1 egg
Pinch salt
Serves: 8

double this for oor lot

Sieve the flour into a large bowl. Add salt. Crack the egg into the centre of the flour. Add about a third of the milk and whisk well with a balloon whisk. Gradually add the rest of the milk and leave to stand for about 30 minutes.

Heat a large frying pan and add some oil. Once very hot, pour out the excess oil. Pour in one ladle full of batter and cook till bubbles form on surface. Flip or turn over and cook other side.

Serve hot, sprinkled with lemon juice and sugar.

We ♥ PancaKes

Scots Sayings

"To pit someone's gas at a peep"

To destroy someone's enthusiasm by putting them in their place. The saying originates from cookery. To reduce the setting on the stove to its lowest, i.e. "pit the gas at a peep or the porridge will boil ower".

FEBRUARY 2013

MONDAY

4
Holiday (NZ: Nelson)

TUESDAY

5
Death of Thomas Carlyle, satirist and historian, 1881.
Birth of John Boyd Dunlop, inventor, 1840

WEDNESDAY

6
Waitangi Day, holiday (NZ)

THURSDAY

7
Death of Lewis Grassic Gibbon (James Leslie Mitchell), 1935

FRIDAY

8
Execution of Mary, Queen of Scots, 1587

SATURDAY

9

SUNDAY

10
Chinese New Year (Year of the Snake).
Murder of John "Red" Comyn by Robert the Bruce, 1306.
Murder of Henry, Lord Darnley, 1567.
Foundation of the University and King's College of Aberdeen, 1495

Doon the watter.

FEBRUARY 2013

MONDAY

11

Death of John Buchan, novelist, historian and Unionist politician, 1940

TUESDAY

12

Shrove Tuesday, last Tuesday before the sacrifices of Lent; also known as Fastern's E'en, Bannock Night, Beef Brose and Shriften E'en.
Fastern's E'en Ba', Duns

WEDNESDAY

13

Ash Wednesday, Lent begins.
Death of Kenneth I, King of Picts, 858.
Massacre of Glencoe, 1692.
Birth of Lewis Grassic Gibbon (James Leslie MItchell), 1901

THURSDAY

14

St Valentine's Day.
Callants Ba', Jedburgh

FRIDAY

15

Vasant Panchami, Hindu festival

SATURDAY

16

SUNDAY

17

Robert the Bruce's tomb discovered, Dunfermline, 1818

"Muckle heid, little wit."

FEBRUARY 2013

MONDAY

18

Holiday (Can: AB, ON, SK, MB).
Washington's Birthday/Presidents' Day, holiday (US)

TUESDAY

19

WEDNESDAY

20

THURSDAY

21

Death of James I, King of Scots, 1437

FRIDAY

22

Heritage Day, holiday (Can: YT).
Death of David II, King of Scots, 1371

SATURDAY

23

SUNDAY

24

Purim, Jewish holiday (from sunset of 23rd)

"A guid man maks a guid wife."

MONDAY

25

TUESDAY

26

WEDNESDAY

27

Battle of Ancrum Moor, 1545.
Death of John Arbuthnot, physician, writer and humorist, 1735

THURSDAY

28

Candlemas, quarter day, Scotland
The National Covenant subscribed, 1638

FRIDAY

1

St David's Day (Wales).
Whuppity Scoorie, Lanark (Spring celebration, where children chase the bad spirits from the town).
Death of Niel Gow, musician, 1807

SATURDAY

2

Birth of Robert II, King of Scots, 1316

SUNDAY

3

Death of Robert Adam, architect and designer, 1792.
Birth of Alexander Graham Bell, scientist, inventor, engineer, 1922

fechtin: fighting.

I love a guid dryin' day.
This wisnae ane.

This
wisnae ane
either.

THE WASHING

They that wash on Monday,
  Hae a' the week to dry ;
They that wash on Tuesday,
  Are no' far by.
They that wash on Wednesday,
  Get their claes clean;
They that wash on Thursday,
  Are no' sair to mean.

They that wash on Friday,
  Washes for need;
But they that wash on Satur-
  day,
  Are dirty daws indeed!

THE DATE OF EAST...

First comes Candlema...
An syne the new meen.
The first Tuesday aifte...
Is Fastern's Een.
That meen oot,
An the neist meen's hic...
On the first Sunday aif...
Is Pess richt.

Oot for tea for
Mither's Day

SCOTS PHRASES

No 109
"The Teuchat's Storm"
This phrase describes unseasonal wintery weather in March said to herald the arrival of the lapwing. This ~~..~~ and obsolete expres-

MONDAY

4

Labour Day, holiday (Aus: WA).
Death of Flora MacDonald, 1790.
Forth Railway Bridge opened, 1890

TUESDAY

5

Birth of David II, King of Scots, 1324

WEDNESDAY

6

THURSDAY

7

FRIDAY

8

Birth of Kenneth Grahame, writer, 1859

SATURDAY

9

SUNDAY

10

Mothering Sunday.
Maha Shivaratri, Hindu festival.
Canadian Daylight Saving begins

glegness: cleverness.

MARCH 2013

MONDAY **11**	Holiday (NZ: Taranaki. Aus: VIC, ACT, TAS). Commonwealth Day. Death of Sir Alexander Fleming, biologist and pharmacologist, 1955
TUESDAY **12**	
WEDNESDAY **13**	Scottish Football Association formed, 1873
THURSDAY **14**	Glasgow subway opened, 1896
FRIDAY **15**	
SATURDAY **16**	
SUNDAY **17**	St Patrick's Day (Ireland). Assassination of Lulach, King of Scots, stepson of Macbeth, 1058. Birth of James IV, King of Scots, 1473. Death of David Dale, founder of New Lanark, businessman and philanthropist, 1806

glaikit: stupid.

MARCH 2013

MONDAY

18
St Patrick's Day, holiday (R of I, NI)

TUESDAY

19
Death of Alexander III, King of Scots, when he falls from his horse at Kinghorn,1286.
Birth of David Livingstone, missionary and explorer, 1813

WEDNESDAY

20

THURSDAY

21

FRIDAY

22

SATURDAY

23

SUNDAY

24
Palm Sunday

"Whaur there's a Jock there's a Jenny."

MARCH 2013

MONDAY

25

Holiday (NZ: Otago).
Old New Year.
Death of Kenneth III, King of Scots, 1005.
Robert the Bruce crowned King of Scots, 1306

TUESDAY

26

Passover begins (from sunset of 25th)

WEDNESDAY

27

Holi, Hindu festival.
Birth of Marion Angus, poet, 1865.
Death of James VI, King of Scots, 1625

THURSDAY

28

Maundy Thursday

FRIDAY

29

Good Friday, holiday (except R of I).
Death of Sir William Burrell, shipping merchant and philanthropist, 1958

SATURDAY

30

Easter Saturday, Lent ends

SUNDAY

31

Easter Sunday.
British Summer Time (BST) begins.
Irish Standard Time (IST) begins

queyn, or quine: a girl.

"The Gowk's Storm" is a period of around three days of chill weather in April associated with the arrival of the cuckoo.

THE CUCKOO

The cuckoo is a bonnie bird,
   He sings as he flies;
He brings us good tidings
   He tells us no lies.

He drinks the cold water
   To keep his voice clear;
And he'll come again
   In the Spring of the year.

PICNICS

Sandwich checklist

1 Use firm, fresh bread (not too soft or crumbly).
2 A sliced loaf gives approx 26 slices and will need around 200g of butter to spread.
3 If posh, remove the crusts, but only when the sandwiches are made up, it makes the edges neater and you can cut several at once.
4 Home-made sandwich spreads can be easily made and are much cheaper than bought ones. Use cream cheese, mayonnaise or hummus as a vehicle for other ingredients: e.g. roast peppers and cream cheese, egg mayonaise with red onions, roast red onions and hummus, cheese savoury (grated cheese and mayonnaise), home made coronation chicken (with mango chutney, mayonnaise and curry powder). Season them well.
5 If you are having meat or fish sandwiches at your picnic ensure you keep them cool in a cool bag till you come to eat them.
6 Consider using flatbreads and wraps for a little variety.

April

April showers mah' May flowers.

APRIL 2013

MONDAY

1

*Dinna laugh, an'
dinna smile BUT hUnT
The gowk anotheR mile*

Easter Monday, holiday (except parts of Scot).
April Fool's Day, Huntigowk

TUESDAY

2

Easter Tuesday, holiday (Aus: TAS).
Passover ends.
Preen-tail Day or Tailie Day [tails were attached to the backs of unsuspecting people as a joke]

WEDNESDAY

3

Scottish Insurrection begins, 1820

THURSDAY

4

Death of John Napier, mathematician and physicist, 1617.
Death of Robert III, King of Scots, 1406

FRIDAY

5

SATURDAY

6

Tartan Day (Can, US).
Declaration of Arbroath signed, 1320

SUNDAY

7

Daylight Saving Time ends (Aus most locations, NZ)

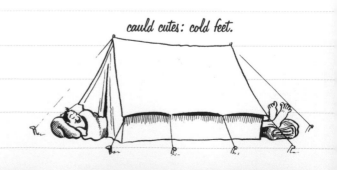
cauld cutes: cold feet.

APRIL 2013

MONDAY

8

Feast of the Annunciation (the announcement to the Virgin Mary that she would conceive)

TUESDAY

9

Vimy Ridge Day (Can)

WEDNESDAY

10

Birth of James V, King of Scots, 1512

THURSDAY

11

FRIDAY

12

SATURDAY

13

Death of Donald I, King of Picts, 862.
Death of Muriel Spark, writer, 2006

SUNDAY

14

"A guid wife and health is a man's best wealth."

APRIL 2013

MONDAY

15

TUESDAY

16

Battle of Culloden, 1746.
Emancipation Day, holiday (US, Washington DC Only)

WEDNESDAY

17

THURSDAY

18

FRIDAY

19

Death of Robert II, King of Scots, 1390

SATURDAY

20

SUNDAY

21

Queen Elizabeth II's Birthday

gowpin: painful, throbbing.

APRIL 2013

MONDAY

22

TUESDAY

23

St George's Day (England).
Death of Alexander I, King of Scots, 1124

WEDNESDAY

24

THURSDAY

25

Anzac Day, holiday (Aus, NZ)

FRIDAY

26

SATURDAY

27

SUNDAY

28

buik-lair: education.

MONDAY

29

TUESDAY

30

Beltane Fire Festival, Calton Hill, Edinburgh

WEDNESDAY

1

Bealltainn / Beltane, Gaelic festival celebrating the arrival of May.
Acts of Union of Scotland and England, 1707.
Death of David Livingstone, missionary and explorer, 1873

THURSDAY

2

FRIDAY

3

SATURDAY

4

Treaty of Edinburgh-Northampton ratified, 1328

SUNDAY

5

twasome: twosome.

May

On May 1st, rise early to wash your face in the May dew

One, Two, Three, Four.
Granpaw at his front door.
Five, six, seven, eight.
Skiving on a chair is great

Rhubarb and Ginger Jam

70

RECIPE CARDS

3 ½ lb rhubarb, chopped
3 ½ lb granulated sugar
Juice of ½ lemon
1 lb crystallised ginger, finely chopped

Wash rhubarb and cut into small pieces.
Put this in alternate layers with sugar
into large earthenware pot. Squeeze
lemon, pour juice into pot and leave
overnight. The next day a good amount
of liquid should have seeped from the
rhubarb. Drain this off into a jelly
pan and boil with preserved ginger for
around 15 minutes. Then add rhubarb
and boil for further fifteen minutes.
After this time, dribble a little onto
a cool plate, let it cool and slide your
finger across it. If it wrinkles it's done.
Remove from heat, skim any scum from
the surface of pot and after around 15
minutes cooling time pour into washed
and sterilised jam pots (that have been
in a cool [100ºC] oven for at least 15
minutes).

Outdoor Family Mag

and of course the
too. It's the subject
conversations, and
the   conversation
the Scots have tr
had a lively way of
their weather. Here
examples:

"the gab o' May": *bad weather
after mid May.*
"The Yowes' Tremmle": *a spell
of cold weather that happens
after the sheep shearing.*
"Rain afore seeven, fair afore
eleeven."

MONDAY

6

Bank Holiday (UK, R of I).
Holiday (Aus: NT, QLD, NSW)

TUESDAY

7

Birth of David Hume, philosopher, 1711.
English soldiers attack and burn Edinburgh, "The Rough Wooing", 1544

WEDNESDAY

8

THURSDAY

9

Birth of JM Barrie, writer, 1860

FRIDAY

10

SATURDAY

11

SUNDAY

12

Gourock Highland Games †.
Mother's Day (Aus, Can, NZ, US)

Event dates marked thus † are to be confirmed. Contact event organisers for details.

drookit: drenched.

MONDAY

13

Battle of Langside, 1568

TUESDAY

14

WEDNESDAY

15

Whitsunday, old Scottish term and quarter day (now 28th).
Shavuot, Jewish holiday, from sunset of 14th

THURSDAY

16

FRIDAY

17

SATURDAY

18

General Assembly of the Church of Scotland begins around this time †

SUNDAY

19

Whit Sunday or Pentecost.
Death of James Boswell, lawyer, diarist, biographer of Samuel Johnson, 1795

lugs: ears.

MONDAY **20**	National Patriots' Day, holiday (Can: QC). Victoria Day, holiday (Scot: Edinburgh; Can except QC)
TUESDAY **21**	
WEDNESDAY **22**	Birth of Sir Arthur Conan Doyle, physician and writer, 1859
THURSDAY **23**	
FRIDAY **24**	Death of David I, King of Scots, 1153
SATURDAY **25**	Atholl Gathering, Blair Castle (Atholl Highlanders' Parade) †. Blackford Highland Games †. West Lothian Highland Games (Bathgate) †
SUNDAY **26**	Trinity Sunday. National Day of Healing (Aus). Atholl Gathering, Blair Castle (Highland Games) †

Event dates marked thus † are to be confirmed. Contact event organisers for details.

"Ane's ain hearth is gold's worth."

MAY/JUNE 2013

MONDAY

27
Memorial Day, holiday (US).
Spring Bank Holiday (UK)

TUESDAY

28
Whitsunday, term and quarter day, Scotland

WEDNESDAY

29

THURSDAY

30

FRIDAY

31
West Linton Whipman Festival begins (till June 8th) †

SATURDAY

1
Bathgate Procession †.
Cornhill, and Shotts Highland Games †.
Lilias Day, Kilbarchan †.
Opening of the first Tay Rail Bridge, 1878

SUNDAY

2
Lanark Lanimer Week begins, (till June 7th) †.
Carrick Lowland Games (Girvan) †.
Markinch Highland Games †

dunt: a hit or a blow.

June

Dingle, dingle, dousy,
The cat's at the well,
Paw's awa' to Musselbro'
To buy the Bairn a bell.

Hush, hush, Bairnie,
And ye'll get a bell
If ye dinna stop greetin'
I'll keep it to masel'.

Paranoid Mother Month...

How to Stop a Toddler Crying

Why does a child cry?
To communicate: hunger, pain, boredom, frustration, a wet nappy, or to get your attention.

If it's boredom or frustration then try these to stop the tears:
- Talking – talk in firm but soothing tones about something to distract them. The subject is not as important as the tone.
- Singing – sing to them; even try to get them to join in if old enough. Combine with a big soothing cuddle.
- Tickling – start off with a nice cuddle then inject some humour into the situation with a tickle!
- Take them outside for a walk.
- Use toys to distract.

Should you give a cuddle or ignore crying?
Don't offer treats to stop tantrums but of course don't ever let your tot cry in real distress without soothing them. How would you feel?

And on no account give them sweeties to stop the crying!

whoops, too late

HEN'S CURES FOR THE HICCUPS

Tickling the Bairn to stop her greetin' gies her the hiccups. Here's whit you can do.

If someone tells her "I'll give you a fiver if you do it again", the shock of this unexpected generosity can cease the hiccups (especially if it's Paw).

Make her laugh - disnae always work but when she hiccups mid-laugh it's quite funny.

Get her to hold her breath, make it a game.

Make her drink water from the opposite side of the glass (as if drinking upside down). This works but is a bit footery for bairns.

Tell her to pat her head and rub her tummy at the same time (doesn't really work but gives me a laugh).

I also find a good big burp can cure the hiccups!

Hiccup, hiccup,
gang away,
Come again
another day;
Hiccup, hiccup,
when I bake,
I'll gie you a
butter cake !

JUNE 2013

MONDAY

3

June Bank Holiday (R of I).
Holiday (Aus: WA; NZ)

TUESDAY

4

WEDNESDAY

5

THURSDAY

6

Lanimer Day, Lanark †

FRIDAY

7

Hawick Common Riding (June 7th–8th) †.
West Linton Whipman (June 7th–8th) †.
Birth of Charles Rennie Mackintosh, artist, designer and architect, 1868.
Death of Robert I, "Robert the Bruce", King of Scots, 1329

SATURDAY

8

Bearsden & Milngavie Highland Games †

SUNDAY

9

Ardrossan, and Forfar Highland Games †.
Guid Nychburris Festival, Dumfries begins (till 15th) †.
Death of St Columba, who brought Christianity to Scotland, 597

Event dates marked thus † are to be confirmed. Contact event organisers for details.

bonnie: beautiful.

MONDAY

10

Holiday (Aus: except QLD, WA)

TUESDAY

11

Death of James III, King of Scots, 1488

WEDNESDAY

12

THURSDAY

13

Birth of James Clerk Maxwell, physicist and mathematician

FRIDAY

14

Selkirk Common Riding Day (festivities from June 7th–15th) †.
Death of John Logie Baird, engineer and inventor, 1946

SATURDAY

15

Guid Nychburris Festival Day, Dumfries †.
Lesmahagow, Newburgh, and Oldmeldrum Highland Games †

SUNDAY

16

Father's Day (Can, R of I, UK, US).
City of Aberdeen Highland Games †.
Peebles Beltane Week begins (till June 22nd) †.
Melrose Festival begins (till June 23rd) †.
Birth of Adam Smith, philosopher and political economist, 1723

ill-trickit: mischievous.

JUNE 2013

MONDAY

17

TUESDAY

18
Riding of Linlithgow Marches †

WEDNESDAY

19
Death of JM Barrie, writer, 1937
Birth of James VI, king of Scots, 1566

THURSDAY

20
Royal Highland Show, Ingliston, begins (till 23rd)

FRIDAY

21
Summer Solstice.
National Aboriginal Day (Can, also local holiday in NWT)

SATURDAY

22
Battle of Bothwell Brig, 1679.
Linlithgow Gala Day †.
Peebles Beltane Festival †

SUNDAY

23
Midsummer E'en.
Galashiels Braw Lads Gathering begins †.
Battle of Bannockburn, first day of battle, 1314

Event dates marked thus † are to be confirmed. Contact event organisers for details.

mither: mother.

JUNE 2013

MONDAY

24

Midsummer Day.
St John the Baptist Day.
Discovery Day (Can: NFL).
La Fête Nationale du Québec (Can: QC).
Battle of Bannockburn, second day and end of battle, 1314

TUESDAY

25

WEDNESDAY

26

Birth of William Thomson, Lord Kelvin, mathematical physicist, 1824

THURSDAY

27

FRIDAY

28

SATURDAY

29

Edinburgh Trades Holiday begins (till July 14th).
Braw Lads Day, Galashiels †.
Ceres, and Drumtochty Highland Games †

SUNDAY

30

Duns Summer Festival begins (till July 6th) †

"Were it not for hope the
heart would break."

July

"HOW TO" N⁰109:
THE HIGHLAND CABER TOSS

Why?
Why toss a caber at all? It might have originated in the need to cross a stream or a moat or something. Now it's a feat of strength performed at Highland Games, and highest marks are for the precision of the throw, the straighter the better.

How big is the caber?
Could be about 20 feet long and from 80 to 180 lbs - depends on what the regulations are for particular games.

How on earth do you even pick up a thing that size?
With difficulty. Even hugely strong guys may need help getting the caber into position just to lift it. Gradually ease the caber onto its tapered end. The thrower bends his knees, with legs more than shoulder-width apart. The upright caber rests against his shoulder. With interlocked fingers he squeezes the caber against himself with the palms of the hand and eases his way down it. When he gets to the tapered end, he squeezes, lifts and then throws it into the air a little – just to get his hands under the end of the caber. He should hold the caber high against the body, elbow height.

What about the throw?
He takes a run, and with a lifting, pulling movement makes the caber fly up into the air, down onto its thicker end and, with skill and luck, the caber should bounce and land pointing perfectly straight.

I've never seen a lassie toss the caber. Do they think it's a daft thing to do?
Women toss the caber too sometimes, it's just a bit smaller than the men's.

Big Daph went to the
lochty Games
Her family went there too
Daphne thocht she'd
got a click
But it wis a heilan coo!

*It was a bull, actually.
I thought I was quite brave!*

Katie Bairdie had a coo,
Black and white aboot the moll',
Washa that a dentie coo?
Dance, Katie Bairdie!

Katie Bairdie had a hen,
Cackled but and cackled ben,
Washa that a dentie hen?
Dance, Katie Bairdie!

JULY 2013

MONDAY

1

Canada Day (Can).
Repeal of the Act of Proscription, 1782

TUESDAY

2

WEDNESDAY

3

Kenmore Highland Games †

THURSDAY

On Bullion's Day, if it be fair,
For 40 days 'twill rain nae mair

4

Independence Day, holiday (US).
Thornton Highland Games †.
Martin of Bullion's day; old Scots festival day to celebrate internment of St Martin's body in Tours Cathedral

FRIDAY

5

SATURDAY

6

Annan Riding of the Marches †.
Forres, Glengarry, Gairloch, and Luss Highland Games †.
Eyemouth Herring Queen Festival (till July 14th, tbc) †.
Birth of John Paul Jones, founder of the US Navy, 1747.
Death of Alexander II, King of Scots, 1249.
Death of Kenneth Grahame, writer, 1932

SUNDAY

7

Cupar Highland Games †.
Death of Sir Arthur Conan Doyle, physician and writer, 1930

Event dates marked thus † are to be confirmed. Contact event organisers for details.

daunder: a stroll.

JULY 2013

MONDAY

8

TUESDAY

9

Nunavut Day, holiday (Can: NU).
Ramadan begins, Muslim observance (from sunset of July 8th).
Birth of Sir William Burrell, shipping merchant and philanthropist, 1861

WEDNESDAY

10

First Bible printed in Scotland, 1579.
Forced abdication of John Balliol, King of Scots, 1296.
Birth of James III, King of Scots, 1451

THURSDAY

11

Birth of Robert I, "Robert the Bruce", King of Scots, 1274

FRIDAY

12

Battle of the Boyne, holiday (NI).
Jethart Callant's Festival Day, Jedburgh †

SATURDAY

13

Fair Saturday, Glasgow Fair Fortnight begins (till July 27th).
Alva, and Morvern Highland Games †.
Opening of the second Tay Rail Bridge, 1887

SUNDAY

14

Stirling Highland Games †

beelin: very angry, red in colour.

JULY 2013

MONDAY

15

Fair Monday, holiday (for some), Glasgow.
St Swithun's Day.
Burntisland Highland Games †

St Swithun's day if it does rain,
For forty days it will remain.
St Swithun's day if it be fair,
For forty days 'twill rain nae mair.

TUESDAY

16

Tisha B'Av, Jewish holiday (from sunset of 15th).
Inveraray Traditional Highland Games †

WEDNESDAY

17

Death of Adam Smith, philosopher and political economist, 1790

THURSDAY

18

Mull Highland Games †.
Death of John Paul Jones, founder of the US Navy, 1792

FRIDAY

19

Cleikum Ceremony and St Ronan's Border Games (till July 20th) †.
Battle of Halidon Hill, 1333

SATURDAY

20

City of Inverness, Lochcarron, Lochearnhead, Taynuilt and Tomintoul Highland Games †.
Comrie Fortnight begins (till August 3rd) †.
Kelso Civic Week begins, (till July 27th)

SUNDAY

21

Stonehaven Highland Games †.
Castle Douglas Civic Week begins (till July 27th) †.
Death of Robert Burns, poet, 1796

Event dates marked thus † are to be confirmed. Contact event organisers for details.

scunnered: exasperated.

JULY 2013

MONDAY

22

Battle of Falkirk, 1298

TUESDAY

23

WEDNESDAY

24

Kelso Civic Week Colour Bussing (parade of the town's flag) †

THURSDAY

25

RICOH Women's British Open begins, St Andrews (till July 28th)

FRIDAY

26

Durness Highland Gathering †.
Langholm Common Riding †

SATURDAY

27

Douglas Day, Castle Douglas Civic Week †.
Countryside Festival, Glamis Castle (till July 28th) †.
Callander, Dufftown, Hallkirk, Lochaber, and Strathconon Highland Games †.
Battle of Killiecrankie, 1689

SUNDAY

28

Lauder Common Riding, events begin (till August 3rd) †.
St Andrews Highland Games †

gowf: golf.

JULY/AUGUST 2013

MONDAY

29

Coronation of James VI, King of Scots, aged only 13 months, 1567

TUESDAY

30

WEDNESDAY

31

Arisaig Highland Games †.
"Poems Chiefly in the Scottish Dialect", the Kilmarnock edition, by Robert Burns, published 1786

THURSDAY

1

Lammas, old Scottish quarter day (now 28th); Lammas is the first harvest festival of the year.
Wearing of Tartan prohibited by the Act of Proscription, 1747.
University of Dundee becomes independant, 1967

FRIDAY

2

Dornoch Highland Games †.
Death of Alexander Graham Bell, scientist, inventor, engineer, 1922

SATURDAY

3

Laylat al-Qadr (Muslim Night of Power).
Lauder Common Riding †.
Aberlour & Strathspey, Aboyne, Brodick, Dundonald, Mey, Inverkeithing, and Newtonmore Highland Games †.
Death of James II, King of Scots,1460

SUNDAY

4

Bridge of Allan, and Montrose Highland Games †.
Coldstream Civic Week begins (till August 10th) †.
Scottish Alternative Games, New Galloway, Dumfries †

Event dates marked thus † are to be confirmed. Contact event organisers for details.

sonsie: jolly.

Paw Broon he went to sea sea sea
To see what he could see see see
His bunnet blew aff and we all had a laugh
And he fell in the deep blue sea sea sea

The Weekly Blether - Issue 342

Home-Made Lemonade

6 large lemons
5 oz sugar
2 ½ pints water

Wash the lemons. Grate zest from lemons. Juice the lemons. Add zest, juice and sugar to a bowl. Boil the water then pour into bowl. Cover and leave overnight. Stir and taste. Add more sugar if you wish. Chill and serve over ice.

OUTWARD BOUND MAGAZINE

STAY SAFE AT THE SEASIDE

- Wear a good quality sunblock with an SPF of above 15.
- Stay in the shade. Sand can reflect UV radiation so take care if you're using a sun shade on the beach, you might still burn.
- It's possible to buy sun tents to help your kids play safely on the beach in the shade.
- Limit outdoor activities to early morning or late afternoon.
- Don't be fooled, the sun's rays can still permeate cloudy skies and burn you. Wear sunblock even if it's cloudy.
- Wear sunglasses to protect your eyes and wear a sun hat to protect your scalp and neck.
- Re-apply sunblock regularly. Do so at least every two hours, and more often if you have been swimming or sweating.
- Don't forget the tip of your nose and your ears, your eyelids, your feet and your shoulders.
- For your lips you must use products designed specifically for them.
- It is not recommended to use sunscreen on children under 6 months of age (they are too susceptible to chemicals at this age) but instead keep them completely out of the sun. When outside use a canopy, a hat, and dress them in specialist sun protective clothing.
- Toddlers should wear long-sleeved, long-legged, sun-protection swimwear.

August

Row, row, row
   your boat
Gently out to sea
Merrily, merrily,
  merrily, merrily
We'll be home
   for tea

AUGUST 2013

MONDAY

5

Summer Bank Holiday (Scot, R of I).
Holiday (Can: most areas. Aus: NT)

TUESDAY

6

Birth of Sir Alexander Fleming, biologist and pharmacologist, 1881

WEDNESDAY

7

Isle of Skye, and Killin Highland Games †

THURSDAY

8

Eid al-Fitr (Ramadan ends).
Ballater Highland Games †.
Coldstream Flodden Cavalcade †.
Tain Highland Gathering †

FRIDAY

9

Assynt, Atholl & Breadalbane (till 10th), Highland Games †.
The Procession of the Burryman, South Queensferry †

SATURDAY

10

Abernethy, Dundonald, North Berwick, and Strathpeffer Highland Gatherings and Games †.
Ferry Fair Festival, South Queensferry †.
The Borders Gathering begins (till 11th) †

SUNDAY

11

Cortachy, and Perth Highland Games †.
Birth of Christopher Murray Grieve, "Hugh MacDiarmid", poet, 1892.
Death of Andrew Carnegie, industrialist and philanthropist, 1919

freends: friends.

AUGUST 2013

MONDAY

12
The "Glorious Twelfth", grouse shooting begins.
Beginning of the visit of King George IV to Scotland, 1822, at Sir Water Scott's suggestion; the pageants were the beginning of a newfound Scots national identity through the wearing of kilts and tartan

TUESDAY

13
Birth of John Logie Baird, engineer and inventor, 1888

WEDNESDAY

14
University of Strathclyde constituted, 1964.
Death of Duncan I, King of the Scots, 1040

THURSDAY

15
Marymass, the Scottish name for feast of the assumption of the Virgin Mary.
Birth of Sir Walter Scott, writer, 1771.
Birth of James Keir Hardie, politician, 1856.
Death of Macbeth, King of the Scots, 1057

FRIDAY

16
Gold Cup Parade (Can: PEI).
Birth of Elsie Inglis, doctor and suffragist, 1864.
Birth of Carolina Nairne, Lady Nairne, songwriter, 1766

SATURDAY

17
Marymass Festival begins, Irvine †.
Bute, Helmsdale & District, Rannoch, and Nairn Highland Games †.
Sanquhar Riding of the Marches †

SUNDAY

18
Caithness, Crieff, and Glenfinnan Highland Games †.
Death of Marion Angus, poet, 1946.
Opening of the Tay Road Bridge, 1966

Event dates marked thus † are to be confirmed. Contact event organisers for details.

dicht/dight: to wipe.

AUGUST 2013

MONDAY

19

TUESDAY

20

WEDNESDAY

21

THURSDAY

22

Argyllshire Gathering (Includes Oban Games) †

FRIDAY

23

Execution of William Wallace, 1305

SATURDAY

24

Wallace Day, Elderslie †.
Lonach Highland Gathering and Games †.
First Edinburgh International Festival, 1947.
Birth of Alexander II, King of Scots, 1198

SUNDAY

25

Grantown-on-Spey Highland Games †.
Death of David Hume, philosopher, 1776.
Death of James Watt, engineer, 1819

tapsalteerie: upside down.

MONDAY

26

Summer Bank Holiday (UK except Scot).
Birth of John Buchan, novelist, historian and Unionist politician, 1875

TUESDAY

27

WEDNESDAY

28

Lammas, quarter day, Scotland.
Founding of St Andrews University, 1413

THURSDAY

29

Cowal Highland Gathering begins (till 31st) †.
Evacuation of St Kilda, 1930

FRIDAY

30

SATURDAY

31

Birnam, Glenurquhart, Invergordon, and Strathardle Highland Gatherings and Games †.
Largs Viking Festival begins (till September 8th) †

SUNDAY

1

Father's Day (Aus, NZ).
Blairgowrie & Rattray Highland Games †.
Birth of Violet Jacob, writer and poet, 1863

Event dates marked thus † are to be confirmed. Contact event organisers for details.

but an' ben: a two-roomed house.

Paw's Boolin' tips

Practice - That's where I've got the upper
hand ower Granpaw. Oh, and talent.
A level head - I don't react to sneaky tactics
like when Jock Reid blaws his big nose whenever
I take a running shot.
Motivation - I want to win!

Know your weaknesses (and, if you are the Skip
like me, those of your team) - In practice
sessions I set up the bools for shots where
we're weakest and go over and over them.
Have a game plan for the whole team.

Stance - Face your target, flex the knees,
balance your weight over both feet (a guid
portion of breid and butter pudding in yer
tummy helps weigh you doon), relax. Swing your
delivery arm towards your eye (not all the way
mind). Don't forget to breathe.

Prizes - If you don't win, at least ye can
enjoy a wee dram wi' yer team-mates in the club
efter.

BLACKBERRY

APPLES

September

As the day lengthens,
The cold strengthens

MONDAY

2

Labor/Labour Day, holiday (US, Can)

TUESDAY

3

WEDNESDAY

4

Forth Road Bridge first opened, 1964

THURSDAY

5

Rosh Hashanah, Jewish New Year, begins (from sunset of 4th)

FRIDAY

6

Rosh Hashanah ends

SATURDAY

7

Braemar Gathering †

SUNDAY

8

Peebles Highland Games †

Event dates marked thus † are to be confirmed. Contact event organisers for details.

piece: a packed lunch, a sandwich.

SEPTEMBER 2013

MONDAY

9

Ganesh Chaturthi, Hindu festival.
Death of Christopher Murray Grieve, "Hugh Mac Diarmid", poet, 1978.
Death of Violet Jacob, writer and poet, 1946.
Death of James IV, King of Scots, 1513, killed in battle at Flodden.
Battle of Flodden, 1513, 500th Anniversary.

TUESDAY

10

Battle of Pinkie, 1547

WEDNESDAY

11

Battle of Stirling Bridge, 1297.
Birth of Mungo Park, explorer, 1771

THURSDAY

12

FRIDAY

13

SATURDAY

14

Pitlochry Highland Games †.
Yom Kippur, Jewish Day of Atonement (from sunset of 13th)

SUNDAY

15

wheech: whoosh.

SEPTEMBER 2013

MONDAY

16

Edinburgh Autumn Holiday

TUESDAY

17

WEDNESDAY

18

THURSDAY

19

FRIDAY

20

Prince Charles Edward Stuart leaves Scotland, never to return, 1746

SATURDAY

21

International Day of Peace.
Invercharron Traditional Highland Games †.
Battle of Prestonpans, 1745.
Death of Sir Walter Scott, writer, 1832.
Birth of John Loudon McAdam, engineer and road builder, 1756

SUNDAY

22

Event dates marked thus † are to be confirmed. Contact event organisers for details.

bowfin': smelly.

SEPTEMBER 2013

MONDAY

23

Holiday (NZ: Canterbury [South])

TUESDAY

24

WEDNESDAY

25

Solemn League and Covenant between England and Scotland passed, 1643

THURSDAY

26

The Queen Mary liner launched at Clydebank, 1934.
Death of Margaret, Maid of Norway, 1290, leaving no obvious heir to the Scots Crown which led to the wars of Scottish Independence.
Death of James Keir Hardie, politician, 1915

FRIDAY

27

Glasgow September Weekend holiday begins (till 30th)

SATURDAY

28

Michaelmas Eve (celebrated by baking a St Michael's Cake, a bannock for Michaelmas Day)

SUNDAY

29

Michaelmas Day (marks the end of harvest time, and you may eat your St Michael's Cake).
New Zealand's Daylight Saving Time begins

pliskie: a prank or a joke.

SEPTEMBER/OCTOBER 2013

MONDAY

30

Queen's Birthday, holiday (Aus: WA)

TUESDAY

1

WEDNESDAY

2

Battle of Largs, 1263, 750th Anniversary

THURSDAY

3

FRIDAY

4

Death of Joseph Bell, surgeon and inspiration for Sherlock Holmes, 1911

SATURDAY

5

Navratri begins, Hindu festival

SUNDAY

6

Australian Daylight Saving Time begins (most locations)

craw: to boast.

THE BARN OWL

ET'S FILTERLESS

A Broons Halloween, by Joe

Guising — nae fancy costumes — just auld claes and a bit o' imagination. An nae sweeties unless ye dae a turn — nane of this "trick or treat" nonsense. Ye say "the sky is blue the grass is green please may I hae my Halloween?" and then ye tell a joke or sing a wee song or, like Horace, recite a whole play.

Neep Lanterns — pumpkins urnae Scottish, neeps are. It's harder work to hollow it out of course. A neep is a big orange swede.

A Pairsty! — Here's whit ye dae:

Dook for Aipples — you try and get aipples oot o' a bath or a basin o' watter using yer teeth. Or — if ye have wallies, or are mibbes feart o' other folk's sleuvers, drap a fork frae yer mooth and spear an aipple that way.

Eat Treacle Scones — Soda scones spread wi treacle are hung tae strings. Wi' yer haunds ahint yer back ye have tae try to eat the scones as they swing aboot, getting stuck tae yer hair and dripping on yer claes. I wonder wha' thocht that up? Probably a dry cleaner.

Eat Clootie Dumplin' — tae be honest us Broons eat clootie dumplin' at a' oor pairsties.

MONDAY

7 Labour Day, holiday (Aus: ACT, NSW, SA).
Queen's Birthday, holiday (Aus: QLD)

TUESDAY

8

WEDNESDAY

9

THURSDAY

10 World Porridge Day

FRIDAY

11 Royal National Mod 2013 begins (till 19th), Paisley

SATURDAY

12 Birth of James Ramsay MacDonald, first Labour Prime Minister, 1866

SUNDAY

13 Navratri ends

scud: a blow.

MONDAY

14

Columbus Day, holiday (US).
Thanksgiving Day (Can)

TUESDAY

15

Eid al-Adha, Muslim festival of sacrifice.
Birth of Allan Ramsay, poet, 1686

WEDNESDAY

16

Birth of James II, King of Scots, 1430

THURSDAY

17

FRIDAY

18

Lukemas, St Luke's Day (patron saint of artists).
Sour Cakes Day, Rutherglen, thin breads of sour dough baked on the eve of St Luke's day were eaten

SATURDAY

19

SUNDAY

20

drouthy: thirsty.

OCTOBER 2013

MONDAY

21

TUESDAY

22

WEDNESDAY

23

The "Auld Alliance", treaty made between Scotland and France, 1295.
Death of John Boyd Dunlop, inventor, 1921

THURSDAY

24

FRIDAY

25

Holiday (NZ: Hawkes Bay).
Mary, Queen of Scots, sentenced to death for alleged treason, 1586

SATURDAY

26

Death of Carolina Nairne, Lady Nairne, songwriter, 1845

SUNDAY

27

British Summertime (BST) ends.
Irish Standard Time (IST) ends

guisers: those who dress up at Halloween, to go out guising (trick or treating).

OCTOBER/NOVEMBER 2013

MONDAY

28
Labour Day, holiday (NZ).
October Bank Holiday (R of I)

TUESDAY

29
Birth of James Boswell, lawyer, diarist and biographer of Samuel Johnson, 1740

WEDNESDAY

30

THURSDAY

31
Halloween.
Samhain, Celtic New Year, autumn harvest festival

FRIDAY

1
All Saints' Day

SATURDAY

2
All Souls' Day

SUNDAY

3
Canadian Daylight Saving Time ends (most locations).
Diwali, Hindu festival of lights, begins

"The sky is blue, the grass is green,
please may we have oor Halloween?"

No 11 MACDUFF'S
SCOTTISH FOODS OF QUALITY

1 lb steak
1 oz dripping
Salt and pepper
¾ pint water
1 oz flour
1 carrot
1 onion
¼ turnip

Stuffing
2 oz breadcrumbs
1 tsp chopped parsley
1 oz chopped suet
Salt and pepper
Milk to bind

Mix stuffing to a stiff paste. Cut steak into strips
2 in wide. Tenderise by hitting with a tenderiser or
a rolling pin. Put 1 tsp stuffing on each and roll
up. Tie with string. Brown well in hot fat. Put in
pot with water and simmer ¾ hour. Add chopped
vegetables and cook ¾ hour or till tender. Remove
string, before serving with boiled vegetables.

Beef Olives

*November's sky is
chill and drear,
November's leaf is red and
sear (withered)*

Rainy Rainy Rattle Stanes,
    dinna Rain on me
Rain on johnnie GRoaT's hoose
    FaR oweR The sea

November

NOVEMBER 2013

MONDAY

4

Holiday (NZ: Marlborough).
Recreation Day, holiday (Aus: Northern TAS)

TUESDAY

5

Muharram, first month of the Islamic Calendar, begins (from sunset of 4th).
Guy Fawkes Night (UK): the gunpowder plot, 1605.
Death of James Clerk Maxwell, physicist and mathematician, 1879.
Birth of Margaret MacDonald Mackintosh, artist, 1865

WEDNESDAY

6

THURSDAY

7

Diwali ends

FRIDAY

8

SATURDAY

9

Death of James Ramsay MacDonald, first Labour Prime Minister, 1937

SUNDAY

10

Remembrance Sunday

clour: a swelling that follows a blow.

NOVEMBER 2013

MONDAY

11

Remembrance Day.
Bank holiday (Can except ON, QC).
Veterans' Day, holiday (US).
Martinmas, old Scottish term and quarter day (now 28th); feast celebrating the completion of autumnal crop seeding and slaughter of farm animals

TUESDAY

12

WEDNESDAY

13

Birth of Robert Louis Stevenson, writer, 1850.
Death of Malcolm III, King of Scots, and also his eldest son Edward, in battle, 1093

THURSDAY

14

FRIDAY

15

Holiday (NZ: Canterbury)

SATURDAY

16

Death of Saint Margaret, Queen Margaret of Scotland, wife of Malcolm III, 1093

SUNDAY

17

syne: rinse, wash out.

NOVEMBER 2013

MONDAY

18

TUESDAY

19

WEDNESDAY

20

THURSDAY

21
Death of James Hogg, poet and novelist, 1835

FRIDAY

22

SATURDAY

23

SUNDAY

24
Battle of Solway Moss, 1542.
Death of John Knox, leader of the Protestant Reformation, 1572

gemme: game.

NOVEMBER/DECEMBER 2013

MONDAY

25

Birth of Andrew Carnegie, industrialist and philanthropist, 1835.
Death of Malcolm II, King of Scots, 1034.
Death of John Balliol, former King of Scots, 1314

TUESDAY

26

Death of John Loudon McAdam, engineer and road builder, 1836.
Death of Elsie Inglis, doctor and suffragist, 1917

WEDNESDAY

27

THURSDAY

28

Hanukkah, Jewish festival of lights, begins (from sunset of 27th).
Thanksgiving Day, holiday (US).
Martinmas, term and quarter day, Scotland.
Battle of Rullion Green, 1666.

FRIDAY

29

SATURDAY

30

St Andrew's Day.
First international association football match between Scotland and England, 1872 (0–0).
Crowning of John Balliol, King of Scots, 1292

SUNDAY

1

Advent Sunday

bummle: sing badly.

December

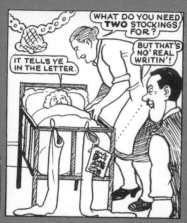

Tipsy Laird

6 small sponge cakes
Raspberry jam
5 oz almond biscuits
6 tbsps Drambuie
2 soup bowls of raspberries
1 pint of custard
10 fl oz double cream
Flaked almonds for topping

Spread sponges with jam
and place in bottom of trifle
bowl. Break up almond
biscuits and sprinkle over
sponges. On top of this pour
6 tbsps Drambuie. On top
of this spread the raspberries. If custard cooled pour
over raspberries and chill.
Spread whipped cream and
cover with flaked almonds.
Serves six.

GROSSET'S FILTERLESS

Whit ye say at somebody's door at
Hogmanay:
My feet's cauld, my shoon's thin ;
Gie's a piece, and let's rin !

DECEMBER 2013

MONDAY

2

Holiday (NZ: Chatham Islands, Westland).
St Andrew's Day, holiday (Scot).
Birth of Joseph Bell, surgeon and inspiration for Sherlock Holmes, 1837.
Birth of Mary Slessor, missionary, 1848

TUESDAY

3

Muharram ends.
Death of Robert Louis Stevenson, writer, 1894

WEDNESDAY

4

Birth of Thomas Carlyle, satirist and historian, 1795.
Death of William I, "The Lion", King of Scots, 1214

THURSDAY

5

Hanukkah ends

FRIDAY

6

St Nicholas Day (patron saint of sailors, merchants, children, and students, and origin of Santa Claus story)

SATURDAY

7

SUNDAY

8

Birth of Mary, Queen of Scots, 1542

langsome: slow and tedious.

MONDAY

9

Death of Malcolm IV, "The Maiden", King of Scots, 1165, aged only 24

TUESDAY

10

Death of Charles Rennie Mackintosh, artist, designer and architect, 1928

WEDNESDAY

11

Anniversary of the Statute of Westminster (Can)

THURSDAY

12

FRIDAY

13

Death of Alexander Selkirk, sailor, inspiration for Robinson Crusoe, 1721

SATURDAY

14

Death of James V, King of Scots, 1542

SUNDAY

15

MSC. X4 COMP. CORE
        X1   STREAM SPEC. MOD.
     X1 OTHER PHM1 MODULE
     X1 STREAM SPEC. PHM2
     X7 ELECTIVE MODULES.

GENERAL

brither: brother.

DECEMBER 2013

MONDAY

16

TUESDAY

17

Death of William Thomson, Lord Kelvin, mathematical physicist, 1907

WEDNESDAY

18

THURSDAY

19

FRIDAY

20

First General Assembly of the Kirk of Scotland, 1560

SATURDAY

21

Winter Solstice

SUNDAY

22

chappin': knocking (can't play)

MONDAY

23

TUESDAY

24

Christmas Eve.
Sowans Nicht (sowans is a dish of oats and fine meal steeped in water).
The beginning of "the daft days" (the days of Yule, between Christmas and Hogmanay)

WEDNESDAY

25

Christmas Day, holiday.
Kirkwall Christmas Ba' Game, Orkney.
The removal of the Stone of Scone from Westminster Abbey, 1950

THURSDAY

26

Boxing Day, holiday (except some areas of Can).
St Stephen's Day, holiday (R of I).
Proclamation Day, holiday (Aus: SA).
Sweetie Scone Day (from the custom of giving sweet scones to neighbours or workers)

FRIDAY

27

St John's Day Mason's Walk, Melrose

SATURDAY

28

Tay Rail Bridge disaster, 1879

SUNDAY

29

daft days: days between Christmas and New Year.

DECEMBER 2013/JANUARY 2014

MONDAY

30

TUESDAY

31

Hogmanay (New Year's Eve).
Biggar's Bonfire.
Comrie Flambeaux Procession.
Stonehaven Fireball Ceremony.
Hawick Reivers Festival.
Birth of Prince Charles Edward Stuart, 1720

Time for a Hogmanay hoolie!

WEDNESDAY

1

Ne'erday, holiday.
Kirkwall New Year Ba' Game, Orkney.
The Loony Dook, South Queensferry.
The Boys' Walk, Dufftown

THURSDAY

2

Holiday (Scot, NZ)

FRIDAY

3

SATURDAY

4

SUNDAY

5

Twelfth Night

"Here's to you and yours, no' forgetting us and oors."

A SELECTION OF
TARTANS OF
SCOTLAND

BLACK WATCH

The Black Watch is an infantry battalion of the Royal Regiment of Scotland. Up until 2006 it was an infantry regiment. This tartan has become a popular choice for even those with no connection to the battalion. It is also known as the "Government sett". It is in use by several military units.

BRODIE

It has been suggested that the Brodies were of Pictish stock, and there is evidence of a Pictish settlement on traditional Brodie territory. The clan name is derived from the Gaelic *brothaig*, meaning a ditch.

BROON

The Broon Clan are said to be of sturdy stock, origin unknown, but the name is common around the towns of Auchenshoogle and Auchentogle and well-known through-out the world. The clan stronghold is Glebe Street with an association with a location known as the But an' Ben.

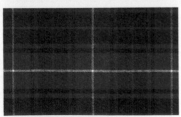

BRUCE

The progenitor of the clan was a Norman knight who travelled to England with William the Conqueror in 1066. Robert de Brus, was a companion-in-arms to King David I, from whom he received lands in Annandale.

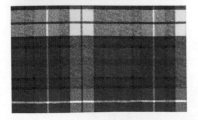

BUCHANAN

The origin of the Buchanans has been traced to Absalon, a steward of the Earl of Lennox around the mid-thirteenth century. "Clarinch" was adopted as the war cry of the Buchanans.

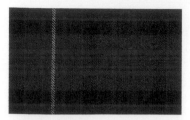

CAMERON

The Camerons had a reputation as a ferocious clan and their war cry, "Sons of the hounds come here and get flesh", reflects this. They were involved in some of the bitterest feuds in clan history.

CAMPBELL

Tradition has it that the clan is descended from Diarmid, a Celtic mythological hero – hence the fact that they are known as the "Race of Diarmid". Historically, their ancestors were certainly of royal stock.

CHISHOLM

The Chisholms are of Norman origin – their name may be derived from Anglo-Saxon meaning "a waterside meadow". The family was well established in the Borders as early as the mid-13th century. The boar's head on the family arms relates to a legend that two Chisholm brothers saved Edward I of England from an attack by a wild boar.

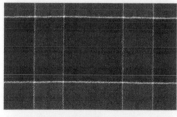

COLQUHOUN

The Colquhouns belonged originally to the Lowlands. There were three branches of the Colquhouns – of that Ilk, of Kilpatrick, and of Luss, which became the principal branch of the family.

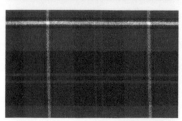

CUNNINGHAM

The Cunninghams trace their descent from one Warnebald, who settled in the district of Cunningham, Ayrshire, obtaining the manor of that name before 1162, and taking his surname from it.

DAVIDSON

The Davidsons appear to have been a Gaelic-speaking clan who lived on lands in Badenoch. In the early part of the fourteenth century the Davidsons became part of the Clan Chattan confederation, an alliance of clans that included the MacPhersons, the MacKintoshes, the MacGillivrays and the MacBeans.

DOUGLAS

The name was derived from Douglas Water in Lanarkshire. Sir William Douglas was governor of Berwick when it was besieged by the English. Douglas was forced to swear loyalty to the English, although he later fought with William Wallace. The line of the Earls of Douglas was extinguished when the ninth Earl forfeited the estates..

DRUMMOND

The origin of the Drummonds is said to be from a younger son of Andrew, King of Hungary (who came over with Edgar Atheling), and his two sisters, one of whom, Margaret, became the wife of Malcolm Canmore. The first recorded chief of the clan was Malcolm Beg, who took the family name from Drymen in Stirlingshire.

ELLIOT

The origins of the Elliotts are somewhat obscure. They appear as an important clan in the south of Scotland in the fifteenth century, but conflicting accounts place their ancestry in the village of Eiot in Forfarshire or around Glen Shee in Angus. The Elliotts took part in many raids on English territory and with their Borders neighbours.

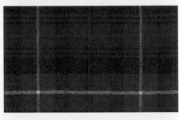

FARQUHARSON

The Farquharsons are of Celtic origin. Their clan country is Strathdee in Aberdeenshire. Some of the clan were originally named Shaw, and it was Farquhar, son of Shaw of Rothiemurchus, who took the name Farquharson. Those families who have an affiliation with the clan include Hardie, MacArdney, MacCuaigh, Grassic, Brebner and Coutts.

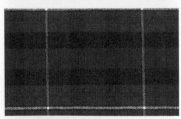

FERGUSON

It is unlikely that there is one common ancestry for the bearers of this name as it is established in many parts of Scotland. The Fergusons of Argyll claim descent from Fergus Mòr, who led his people, the 'Scoti', from Antrim to settle in Argyll and establish the ancient tribal kingdom of Dalriada in the fifth and sixth centuries

FRASER

The name is said to be derived from the town of Fréselière in Anjou and is first found in the south of Scotland in the twelfth century. In 1160 Simon Fraser held lands at Keith in East Lothian. Around 1306, the Frasers left East Lothian and began to establish the clan in Aberdeenshire.

GORDON

The first record of the Gordons places them in the Lowlands and suggests they were of Anglo-Norman origin. The Highland clan is descended from Sir Adam Gordon, a supporter of Robert the Bruce who received the lands of Strathbogie in return for his services to the king. The family built Huntly Castle on these lands in the fifteenth century.

GRANT

The Grants are of Norman stock, originally called 'le Grand', although some claim they are descended from Alpin, the first king of Picts and Scots. By the fourteenth century, the Grants were established as one of the most powerful and influential of the Highland clans. The principal seat of the clan is Castle Grant, near Grantown-on-Spey.

GUNN

Originally this clan was Norse. Their founder is said to have been Gunni, the son of Olaf the Black, the thirteenth-century king of Man and the Isles. Their lands were in the far north, in Caithness and Sutherland. A ferocious, war-like clan (the Norse name *Gunni* meant "war"), the Gunns extended their territory in this area.

HAY

The history of the Hays begins with one William de Haya who was at the court of Malcolm IV. In 1172 he was granted the lands of Errol in Perthshire. It is believed that de Haya was descended from one of the Norman princes who travelled to England with William the Conqueror. William de Haya and his son both married into ancient Scottish stock.

JOHNSTONE

The Johnstones were once the most powerful of the Borders clans, with extensive lands in Annandale. The name is derived from John, the progenitor of the clan, who named the property granted to him 'John's toun' in the twelfth century. The Johnstones had a long and bloody feud with the Maxwells, a powerful clan with lands in Nithsdale.

KENNEDY

The Kennedys travelled from Ireland to the Celtic kingdom of Dalriada. Around the twelfth century, the clan settled on lands in Carrick in Ayrshire and were to dominate this area for many centuries. In the eighteenth century the Kennedy chiefs took up residence at Culzean Castle, designed by Robert Adam, overlooking the Firth of Clyde.

KERR

The Kerrs were one of the great Borders clans and their ancestors were from Normandy. A rivalry between two branches of the family – Ferniehurst and Cessford – existed until the 17th century. Hostility ended in 1631 when they were united through marriage: William Kerr, a descendent of the Kerrs of Ferniehurst, to Anne Kerr of Cessford.

LINDSAY

The Lindsays are of English origin and first appear in the Borders in the early twelfth century. Sir William of Lindsay accompanied King David I on his journey north to claim the Scottish throne. The Lindsays had many distinguished clansmen, one of whom is Sir David Lindsay, Lord of Crawford, who signed the 1320 Declaration of Arbroath.

MACALISTER

The MacAlisters are descended from Alasdair Mòr, son of Donald, Lord of the Isles, great grandson of the mighty Somerled. The clan settled on lands around Tarbert in Argyll, with the chief establishing lands at Loup. in the 18th century the Tarbert lands passed out of their possession. Since that time the chief has lived at Kennox in Ayrshire.

MACAULAY

The MacAulays of Lewis claim descent from the Norse Olaf the Black, while the MacAulays of Argyll are descended from Aulay, the brother or son of a 13th-century Earl of Lennox, and before that from the Clan Alpin. It is said the Lewis MacAulays were originally from Ullapool and were related to the MacAulays of Sutherland and Ross.

MACARTHUR

The family of Arthur is one of the oldest in Argyll which led to the proverb, 'There is nothing older unless the hills, MacArthur and the devil'. It has been claimed that the clan is a branch of the Clan Campbell. Members of a branch of the MacArthurs were for many generations hereditary pipers to the MacDonalds of Sleat, on Skye.

MACCALLUM

The MacCallums first appear in the ancient district of Lorn in the early fifteenth century, when Ranald MacCallum of Corbarron was made hereditary constable of Craignish Castle in 1414. The MacCallum clan adopted a different sett of the tartan in the late 18th or early 19th century, with the blue line of the traditional design replaced by red.

MACDONALD

The most powerful of the Highland clans, the Clan Donald was descended from Donald, grandson of Somerled, Lord of the Isles. The name MacDonald is at the centre of the Massacre of Glencoe of 1692, in which around 40 clan members were slaughtered by a Highland regiment under the command of Robert Campbell of Glenlyon.

MACDOUGALL

The male line of Somerled, Lord of the Isles, d. 1164, was continued in MacDougall, descended from Dugald, eldest son of Somerled. Dugald's lands included most of Argyll and the islands of Mull, Tiree, Coll and Jura. Dugald's son and grandson, Duncan and Ewan, built castles in Argyll, including Dunollie, Duntrune and Dunstaffnage.

MACDUFF

The MacDuffs are the medieval earls of Fife, a title first conferred on Aed, son of Malcolm Canmore. Aed married the daughter of Queen Gruoch, wife of Macbeth. The Earl of Fife held the right to enthrone the king of Scots. The line of the medieval Earls ended with the death of Duncan, in 1353. In 1759 the earldom of Fife returned to the Duff family.

MACFARLANE

The MacFarlanes are descended from the Celtic earls of Lennox, from Gilchrist, the younger son of Alwyn, who lived around the end of the twelfth century. Their name is derived from Gilchrist's great-grandson, Parlan, the Gaelic form of the name Bartholomew. The clan is reputed to have influenced the downfall of Mary, Queen of Scots.

MACGREGOR

Descended from Gregor, a descendant of Kenneth Mac-Alpin. In the 16th century, for 140 years, the MacGregors suffered persecution. Many dispersed and sought shelter with other clans, changing their names. The laws against the clan were repealed in 1774. Rob Roy MacGregor was immortalised in Sir Walter Scott's romantic novel.

MACINNES

One 17th-century historian asserts that the MacInneses, were a branch of the Siol Gillebride, who were the first inhabitants of Morvern and Ardnamurchan. The MacInneses were constables of Kinlochaline Castle. During the 18th and 19th centuries the clan became dispersed, with many members emigrating to the New World.

MACINTYRE

The traditional history of this clan states that they are a sept of the MacDonalds of Sleat, and that their ancestor was one MacArill, a nephew of the great Somerled, Lord of the Isles. The Gaelic form of their name, Mac an t-saoir, means "son of the carpenter", and appropriately the MacIntyres once held the office of foresters to the Lord of Lorn.

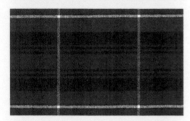

MACKAY

This clan occupied lands in Durness, from the northwest peninsula of Cape Wrath, extending eastward to the border of Caithness and south to the northern edge of Sutherland. The MacKays, originally known as Clan Morgan, are believed to be descendants of the royal house of Moray, one of the seven Celtic earldoms.

MACKENZIE

The clan is of Celtic origin, and goes back to at least the 13th century, when it was established at Eilean Donan, which was to be its stronghold for centuries. Their support of the failed 1715 Jacobite rebellion resulted in the forfeit of lands and titles. The lands were repurchased and the title Earl of Seaforth restored in 1771, but the male line died out in 1815.

MACKINTOSH

Shaw, son of the third Earl of Fife, was awarded lands in Invernesshire in 1163. Assuming the name Mac an Toisich which means "son of the toisech ['thane']" or "son of the Chief", he became the progenitor of his own clan. Moy Castle on Moy Island was the original seat of the chief of Clan Mackintosh. Moy Hall is the current seat.

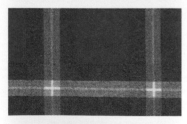

MACLAINE

The ancestor of the MacLaines of Lochbuie was Hector Reaganach, brother of Lachlan Lubanach, ancestor of the MacLeans of Duart. They had great possessions in Mull granted to them by the Lord of the Isles. Clan legend states that the death of a MacLaine is heralded by the headless ghost of Ewan, son of Iain Og, fifth chief, riding through Glen More.

MACLEAN

The MacLeans claim descent from a Celtic warrior, Gillean of the Battleaxe, a kinsman of Fergus Mòr, the sixth-century ruler of the ancient kingdom of Dalriada. The progenitor of the clan was Lachlan Lubanach, who lived in the late fourteenth century. Lachlan was married to the daughter of the first Lord of the Isles and from him received lands in Mull.

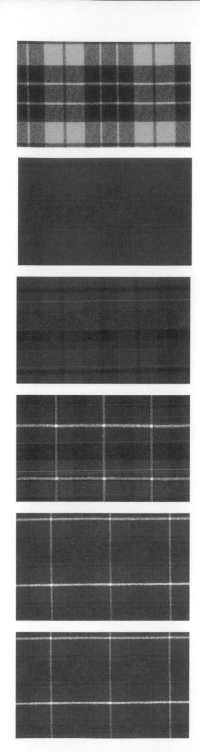

MACLEOD

The MacLeods are Norse, descended from Leod, son of Olaf the Black, King of Man and the Isles. Leod's sons were progenitors of two main branches of the clan – Torquil in Lewis and Tormod in Skye and Harris. Alasdair, eighth chief of Harris, built St Clements Church at Rodel in Harris and the fairy tower at Dunvegan Castle on Skye, ancient seat of the MacLeod chief.

MACNAB

The ancestor of the Clan MacNab is said to have been the powerful Abbot of Glen Dochart and Strathearn, younger son of Kenneth MacAlpin, who flourished in the twelfth century. In 1124 the name was recorded in a charter and the MacNabs appear to have occupied the Glendochart lands from an early period.

MCNAUGHTON

The McNaughtons are of Pictish origin. They are descended from a Pictish king by the name of Nechtan or Nauchton. In the 12th century they possessed lands at Strath Tay in Morayshire and in the following century were granted lands along Loch Awe in Argyll. The clan made their seat at Dunderave and the castle there was built in 1596.

MACNEIL

The MacNeils of Barra and those of Gigha can trace their origin to Neil Og who lived about 1300. The earliest record of a MacNeil of Barra occurs in 1427. In 2001 Kisimul Castle on Barra, the clan stronghold, was leased by America-born Chief Ian Roderick MacNeil to Historic Scotland for 1000 years, for the annual sum of £1 and a bottle of whisky.

MACPHEE

The Gaelic form of this name, MacDubh-Shith – "dark one of peace" – was rendered in English as MacDuffie and variously as Macafee, MacFee, MacFie and MacPhee. The origin of this Colonsay family is unclear. In folklore they are associated with a legend of a seal-woman who married an islander. Their true progenitor may have been a member of the Clan Alpin.

MACQUARRIE

The Clan MacQuarrie is Norse. They first appeared in possession of the island of Ulva and part of Mull. John MacQuarrie of Ulva, d. 1473, is the first MacQuarrie prominently mentioned. Lachlan MacQuarrie, sixteenth and last chief, played host to James Boswell and Samuel Johnson, on their famous tour of the Western Isles in 1773.

MACQUEEN

The name is Norse, derived from Sweyne and is rendered in Gaelic as MacShuibne, from which come the anglicised forms of Sween, MacSween, MacSwan and MacQueen. The Skye branch settled at Garafad, while another branch prospered on the island of Scalpay. Many members of the clan emigrated to North America during the eighteenth century.

MACRAE

Macrae in Gaelic is MacRath, which means "Son of Grace". The home of the "Wild Macraes" was Kintail, where they did great service for the Earls of Seaforth. As Jacobites, the Macraes fought at Sheriffmuir in 1715, and loyally afterwards for the House of Hanover. Major Robert M'Crea fought as a loyalist in the American War of Independence.

MATHESON

The Clan Matheson is of Celtic heritage, from a kinsman of the Lords of Lorn. In the 13th century the clan settled on lands around the Kyle of Lochalsh and Kintail. The two main branches of the clan are descended from Murdoch Buidhe, who lived in the late 16th century. A further branch of the family was established at Shiness in Sutherland.

MENZIES

The name is French, derived from Mesnières in Normandy. Robert de Menyers is recorded as Lord High Chamberlain at the court of King Alexander II. Robert was granted lands in Atholl and Glen Lyon, and his son, Alexander, in Aberfeldy. The Menzies gave their support to Robert the Bruce. The chief at Culdares supported the Jacobite rebellion of 1715.

MORRISON

Meaning "son of Morris", or Maurice, this was a common surname in Middle Ages Scotland and so the name is not confined to one clan in one area. Morrisons were to be found all over mainland Scotland and on Harris and Lewis. The tartan is based on the MacKay sett (with whom the Morrison name has a strong connection), with a red stripe.

MUNRO

In Gaelic Munro is Mac an Rothaich, meaning "Man from Ro", supporting the traditional story that the clan was from the River Roe area in Ireland. Modern evidence has indicated that they may have been Norman in origin. The clan lands were in Ross-shire. Allied clans were Ross, Fraser, MacKay and Sutherland.

MURRAY

The Murrays are Flemish in origin, descended from nobleman Freskin de Moravia, who established himself in Moray at the invitation of the King of Scots. He took the name 'de Moravia', i.e. "of Moray" in Latin. MacMurray, Moray, Murry, Morrow, and Morogh are all variants of the name.

OGILVY/OGILVIE

The Ogilvys take their name from the placename near Glamis, first recorded in about 1205 as Ogilvin. Patrick de Olgilvy appears on the Ragman Roll swearing fealty to King Edward I of England in 1296. Associated family names include Airlie, Findlater, Gilchrist, Macgilchrist, Milne, Richardson and Storie.

OOR WULLIE

Native to Auchenshoogle since 1936, this clan is a group of bonnie fechters. Oor Wullie's clan includes Fat Bob, Soapy Soutar, Wee Eck and Jeemy the moose. His rivals include the Murdoch clan led by the inimitable PC Murdoch, and the Bullies clan led by the infamous Basher McTurk. The clan stronghold is Oor Wullie's Shed.

ROBERTSON (CLAN DONNACHAIDH)

Robertson is one of the oldest of all the Scottish clans. There are two theories as to its origins. One is that its founder is Duncan (Donnachaidh), the second son of Angus MacDonald, Lord of the Isles. That other is that the Robertsons are descendants of the Celtic Earls of Atholl, whose progenitor was Duncan I, eldest son of Malcolm II.

STEWART

The first ancestor of the Royal Race was a Breton noble, Alan. By his second son, William Fitz-Alan, he became ancestor of the Earls of Arundel and Dukes of Norfolk, etc. His third son, Walter Fitz-Alan, received from David I the office of Great Steward of Scotland, and was progenitor of the House of Stewart. The direct male line failed with James V.

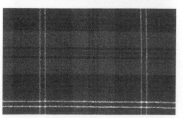

URQUHART

This clan takes its name from the district so-called in Rossshire. The Urquharts of Cromarty at one time possessed nearly all the old county of Cromarty. Thomas Urquhart was Bishop of Ross in 1449, and in 1585 Alexander Urquhart was last Dean of Ross. History makes frequent reference to Sir Thomas Urquhart of Cromarty and his family.

Bread and Butter Pudding

1 egg yolk
1 tablespoon sugar
1/2 (285 ml) pint milk
2 slices thin bread and butter
1 oz (30 g) currants

Dissolve sugar in milk and simmer till sugar dissolved (do not boil). Beat egg yolk in a bowl and add warm milk to the bowl. Return the mixture to pan and simmer, stirring continuously. Do not boil. Strain and set aside. Cut bread and butter into triangles, and lay it in a buttered oven dish. Sprinkle currants in between. Pour custard over bread and let it soak for half an hour. Bake in a moderate-to-hot oven (160°C/320°F) for 30–40 minutes or until the pudding is risen and set. Tip: Use brambles instead of currants for a tasty alternative.

For further information we recommend reading:
The Concise Scots Dialect Dictionary, Alexander Warrack, Waverley Books, Glasgow, 2006.
The Essential Scots Dictionary, Eds. Iseabail Macleod and Pauline Cairns, Edinburgh University Press, Edinburgh, 1996. www.scotsdictionaries.org.uk.
Collins Encyclopedia of Scotland, Eds. John Keay and Julia Keay, HarperCollins Publishers, London, 1994.
150 Famous Scots, Lily Seafield, Waverley Books, Glasgow, 2009.